HOWARD JONES

BY PHILIP KAMIN

Howard Jones, resplendent in his shock of electric red hair. His music has been hailed as the pop of the future.

Produced by
GODDARD & KAMIN INC.
Designed by KEITH ABRAHAM
Separations and film by
IMPERIAL GRAPHICS, Toronto

For Keith

Special thanks to Glenda, Keith, Dave, Steve and everyone at H.L., and to Richard, Ron and Isaac at Monarch Books Canada. Special thanks also to Leo Robichaud, Doug Paddey, Marty Ingles and Gary Beck at Canon Cameras of Canada.

Photographs by Philip Kamin except as follows: Gary Gershoff/Retna, page 3; JF/Retna, front poster, page 25; Lyn McAfee/Retna, page 30; Paul Natkin/StarFile, pages 7 and 20; A.J. Pantsios/StarFile, pages 6, 10, 11, 22 and 23; Chuck Pulin/StarFile, pages 5, 12 and 13; David Redfern/Retna, page 24; Retna, inside front cover and back cover; SFA/Retna, page 2; SL/Retna, pages 9, 16 and 17; StarFile, page 31; Vinnie Zuffante/StarFile, page 27.

robus books
P.O. Box 13819, Wauwatosa, WI, 53213, U.S.A.

Printed in the U.S.A.

ISBN 0-88188-412-X

MEET HOWARD JONES

He plays synthesizers and sports a reddish shock of a haircut that looks as if it might have been the result of a severe electrical accident. He made a name for himself playing solo and singing songs about hope and personal freedom—not about despair and dissatisfaction.

In comparison with many new British artists, Howard Jones is a reactionary, a freak, an aberration. He also sells records by the boxcar load. He's married and leads a fairly normal life, the demands of his career notwithstanding. And he understands pop music is supposed to be uplifting. It's supposed to be fun.

Howard Jones was born to Welsh parents in the British seaport of Southampton in 1954 and in his teens succumbed to restlessness that characterizes his generation.

Actually, before then, it was his father's restlessness that helped shape young Howard's personality. He spent his childhood moving constantly, from house to house and country to country, while his father flipped from one career to another. By the age of 14, Howard and his family had emigrated twice to Canada, and returned twice to Britain.

Committed early in his life to a career in music, Howard moved around the country a great deal, played with a number of unknown bands and eventually, at 19, took to studying classical piano at the Northern School of Music in Manchester.

ABOVE: *Howard Jones, pop prophet or humanist songwriter? He makes no claims on his audience; he just asks his fans to be themselves.*

OPPOSITE: *For years he worked alone on stage with banks of synthesizers. Critics say he "humanized" them, made them warm and unthreatening.*

OPPOSITE: *Born in the British seaport of Southampton, Howard moved from city to city and country to country before he left home in his late teens. His family emigrated twice to Canada and returned twice to Britain before Howard was 14.*

ABOVE: *Howard and his brother Martin, who, with drummer Trevor Morais, became Jones' first touring band in 1985.*

Howard Jones' brand of danceable, optimistic pop has made him a superstar in Europe, North America, Australia, and Japan. It has taken him just two years and two albums to accomplish that, and some people believe he's the "one-man Beatles" of the 1980s.

Keyboard genius, humanist songwriter, charismatic pop star, a responsible married man: Howard Jones contemplates a satisfying life and a rewarding future.

CHRONOLOGY

1979–1981

Disillusioned with the teaching system and the snobbery exhibited by his student colleagues and mentors, he left school and travelled to High Wycombe, Buckinghamshire, in 1979. He lives there still, with Jan, his wife of several years.

He recently gave his first home—a two (rooms) up, two down row house—to his parents, and moved into more elegant digs nearby.

But six years ago, things seemed to be moving slowly for Howard. He drifted directionlessly through a series of jobs—as a factory hand and, with Jan, as a door-to-door fruit and vegetable vendor. For a couple of years he abandoned music entirely.

He did manage, however, to save 250 pounds, enough to buy his first inexpensive synthesizer. He believed from the start that synthesizers were the pop instruments of the future—they're adaptable, affordable, portable, and capable of producing a great variety of musical sounds, he used to say.

And because this often reviled instrument was Howard's only accompaniment on stage in his first pub gigs around High Wycombe, he managed to "humanize" it, to make it warm and expressive, while other performers seemed content to exploit only the synthesizer's cold, robotic, pre-programmed functions.

Years later, Howard's synthesizer work—along with that of veteran U.S. keyboardist Stevie Wonder—would be acclaimed by critics and fans alike for its adventurousness and color.

1982

At those early pub gigs Howard and lyricist William Bryant formulated a unique philosophy: they opted for unsentimental, upbeat songs that encouraged individuality and personal strength in the face of Britain's depressing social, political, and economic climate.

But Howard wouldn't moralize, and he wouldn't preach. Nor would he foist standard political dogma on his fans. His message was spiritual fulfillment, not revolution.

And in High Wycombe Howard first met mime-artist Jed Hoile, a fan who travelled from gig to gig and rose from the audience every night Howard played to illustrate his songs with interpretive dances and broadly-drawn characters.

Their relationship became professional when Howard undertook his first nationwide tour in 1982, and Jed—who has now made a serious study of mime techniques—has been an indispensible part of Howard's performances ever since.

Howard Jones takes a bow after a concert on his 1984 U.S. tour, his shirt ablaze with the colors of every country he has conquered.

1983

Howard Jones' first single, the optimistic/humanistic *New Song* on the WEA U.K. label, was the nation's biggest summer hit, and became an instant success in North America as well. On the strength of that first song and Howard's debut album, **Human's Lib**—both produced by Duran Duran producer Colin Thurston—Jones and Hoile toured North America, selling out 3,000-seat venues without effort.

The media, at first indifferent to the young performer, were won over by his dynamic, theatrical performances. Almost as quickly as he conquered the imagination of the British public, he was also a hit in Canada, Australia, and the United States.

Later that year *New Song* was followed by two other hit singles in Britain—*Conditioning* and *Change The Man.*

Howard takes in the crowd during his performance at The Pier in New York, in April, 1985.

ABOVE: *Howard and mime artist Jed Hoile. Their performance partnership goes back to 1979, when Howard first started playing pubs in High Wycombe.*

OPPOSITE: *By 1985, when this concert shot was taken, Howard had scored seven Top 18 hits in Britain and three in North America.*

Performing at Wembley Arena, 17 April, 1985.

Howard, an artist with great charm…

and extraordinary talent.

"Things Can Only Get Better"...

HOWARD JONES

1984

Consolidating his initial success, Jones undertook a second world tour, this time filling 15,000-seat arenas. By now he'd proved himself to fans. **Human's Lib** had remained on the Top 20 in Britain and Japan for six months.

But a section of the radical British music industry had turned against him, citing his refusal to align himself with any political movement and his vegetarianism as evidence of a basic flakiness, a refusal to deal with realities.

That irked him a little, but he stuck to his guns, maintaining that he just never wanted to belong to any movement and that his diet was nobody's business; he simply doesn't like meat. In fact, he hasn't eaten it for 10 years. Why should it become an issue now?

Howard and Jan Jones also began producing a glossy, well-edited fan magazine, *Risk*, distributed through the fan club administered by Jan.

The magazine offers not just fan information, but recipes (vegetarian, of course!), contests, giveaways, and travel stories.

At the end of 1984, Howard scored two more chart hits—*Like To Get To Know You Well* and *Look Mama.* Both would be included on his second album, **Dream Into Action,** released early in 1985.

He has always had a special affection for Canadian audiences. In fact, Toronto is one of Howard's favorite cities, and on his shirt you'll see he has sewn a little Maple Leaf—a symbol of his friendship with Canadians.

1985 was a big year for Howard. Here he is in concert at Wembley Stadium in London. A few months earlier he'd also filled London's prestigious Albert Hall.

1985

Dream Into Action, produced by Rupert Hine, was intended as further encouragement to the fans attracted to *New Song's* optimism. It's about putting dreams and ideals into concrete action, Howard told the press on its release. It prompted activity in the fulfillment of personal ambitions, not armchair philosophizing.

Spurred by the single *Things Can Only Get Better*, which features a brassy funk arrangement and a full band sound, the album sold well in excess of 1,000,000 copies by the time Jones—and, for the first time, a backing band—toured North America in the early summer.

The band—Howard's brother Martin on bass and drummer Trevor Morais—enhanced Howard's stage presentation without detracting from the essence of his performance, the interaction between his music and Hoile's larger-than-life characterizations.

And the songs on **Dream Into Action**—with lyrics by Howard, who used his experiences touring the U.S. with the Eurythmics as a creative base—offered a more penetrating exploration of the artist's psyche, without resorting to standard love themes and meaningless rock anthems.

Mid-way through 1985, **Dream Into Action** is still one of the year's top sellers, and continues to prove Howard Jones is an artist with great charm and extraordinary talent.

Photo: Giorgio Palmisano

On stage belting out New Song . . . *communing with nature.*

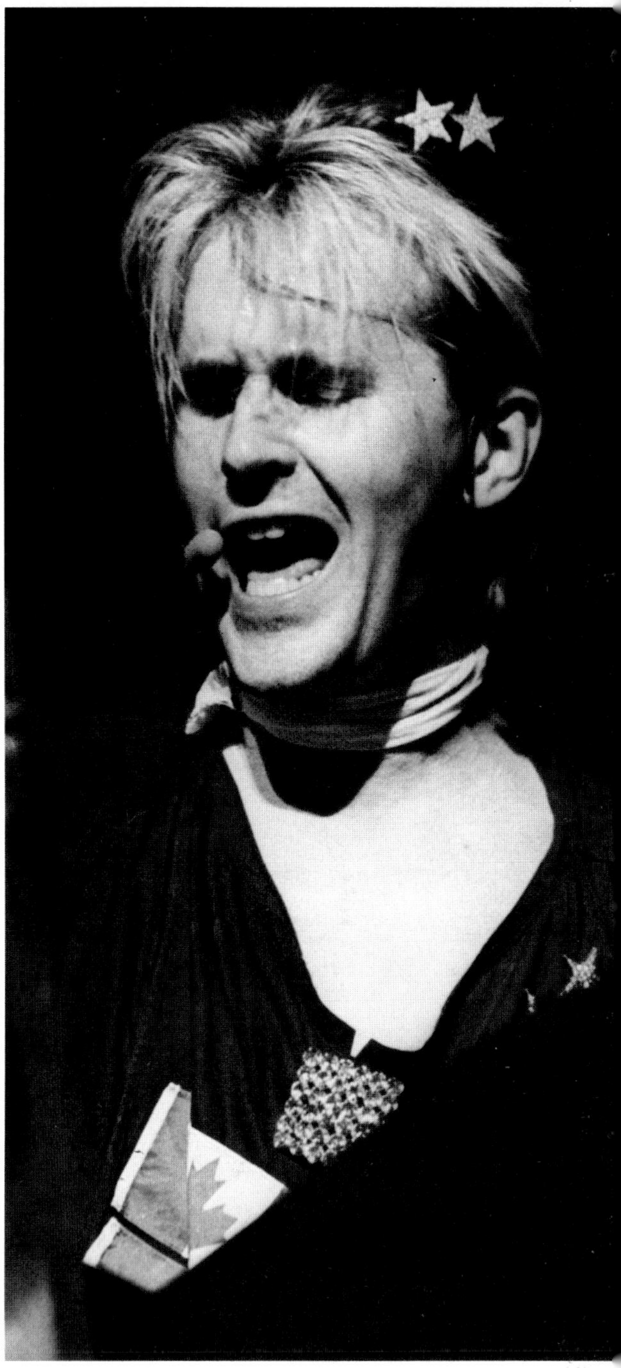

As a solo performer, Howard Jones re-invented a performance mode that was considered impossible since the era of the folksinger. He used technology—synthesizers, wireless microphones, and pre-programmed tape loops—to free himself of the burden of performing with a band.

DISCOGRAPHY

In 1984 Howard Jones won the readers' Poll for the U.S. magazine Keyboard. *It was a distinction the young synthesist celebrated at a special concert in which he played alongside Stevie Wonder.*

SINGLES:

New Song
Conditioning
Change The Man
Like To Get To Know You Well
Look Mama
Things Can Only Get Better
No One Is To Blame
Life In One Day

ALBUMS:

Human's Lib (1983)
Dream Into Action (1985)

How to contact Howard Jones:

In the U.S.A.
Warner Bros. Records
75 Rockefeller Plaza
New York, N.Y., 10019

In Great Britain
WEA Records
20, Broadwick St., London,
W1V 2BH, England

RISK

Howard and Jed: One of the most challenging performance duos in pop history.

OVERLEAF: Howard lays into Look Mama, *a passionate song about the classic struggle between parents and their children, at the Montreux Pop Festival, May, 1985.*

ABOVE: *Howard at a restaurant on his 1985 North American tour. He refuses to eat meat, and his vegetarian diet is detailed in the pages of* Risk, *his fan club magazine.*

OPPOSITE: *On stage he's a carrot-topped dynamo, a blur of fascinating color and emotion. Off stage, however, Howard Jones is just like the rest of us; a dreamer, a quiet thinker, an attentive listener and learner.*

Howard waves his thanks at the end of his winning performance at the Live Aid concert in July. He won't preach to his audience, he says. He only wants to encourage his fans to be strong individuals and to reach out and grasp their dreams.

About the Author:
Philip Kamin began photographing rock bands in 1978 when he picked up a camera for the first time and followed Genesis on tour. Since then his photographs have appeared worldwide in magazines, song-books, programs, publicity campaigns and books, and on album covers and posters. Along with award-winning writer Peter Goddard, Philip has produced books on The Rolling Stones, The Who, David Bowie, The Police, Genesis, Van Halen, Duran Duran, Michael Jackson & the Jacksons, Bruce Springsteen, Wham!, Phil Collins, David Lee Roth, Madonna, Bryan Adams, Tears for Fears, and Paul Young, with books on The Cars and Cyndi Lauper to follow.

Philip Kamin uses **Canon** cameras and equipment exclusively: F1 and A1 bodies with motor drives; lenses: 24mm f/2, 35mm f/2, 50mm f/1.4, 85mm f/1.8, 135mm f/2, 200mm f/1.8, 300mm f/4 Aspherical, 400mm f/4.5 and Canon strobe system.